T

MW01094540

Puerto Rican Drinks

Recipes

17 Authentic Mixed Beverage Recipes Direct from Puerto Rico

By

Grace Barrington-Shaw

More books by Grace Barrington-Shaw:

Disclaimer

All reasonable efforts have been made to provide accurate and error-free recipes within this book. These recipes are intended for use by persons possessing the appropriate technical skill, at their own discretion and risk. It is advisable that you take full note of the ingredients before mixing and use substitutes where necessary, to fit your dietary requirements.

Contents

Introduction

The most popular drink from Puerto Rico is the Pina colada, it is well known around the world and has become Puerto Rico's National beverage. However, there are many more fantastic beverages from Puerto Rico that are hugely popular and just as exciting to taste. Whether alcoholic or non-alcoholic, the drinks in this recipe book are enjoyed by Puerto Rican's around the world.

Most Puerto Rican drinks make use of readily available fruits on the island, as well as coffee that grows wild in much of the hilly terrain. Rum is also heavily featured in many of the cocktails and alcoholic beverages coming out of Puerto Rico. Puerto Rican rum is deemed to be some of the best rums to be found anywhere in the world, just after Cuba.

In this drink recipes book, I highlight the alcoholic, non-alcoholic and hot beverages of Puerto Rico. These are authentic drinks that are popular with natives and Puerto Rican communities around the world. All recipes are in general, quite straight forward to prepare, so you will be able to have fun mixing them for your family and friends, allowing you to become a Puerto Rican bartender in your own rite! Experiment and enjoy the best drinks that Puerto Rico has to offer!

FREE Bonuses

We have 3 **FREE** bonus recipe ebooks for your enjoyment!

- **Cookie Cookbook** 2134 recipes
- **Cake Cookbook** 2444 recipes
- **Mac and Cheese Cookbook** 103 recipes

Simply visit: **www.ffdrecipes.com** to get your **FREE** recipe ebooks.

You will also receive free exclusive access to our World Recipes Club, giving you FREE best-selling book offers, discounts and recipe ideas, delivered to your inbox regularly.

Frappe

This frozen treat is a creamy blend of ice cream, coconut cream, fresh fruit and rum. It bears some similarity to the piña colada however affords greater flexibility with the kind of fruit added. Frappes are a common find all over Puerto Rico and can easily be whipped up at home.

Makes 2 servings

Ingredients

6 oz parcha juice

2 tablespoons coconut cream

½ lb pineapple chunks

1 ripe banana

2 oz white rum

6 big ice cubes

Preparation

1. Place all the ingredients into a blender and blend until the mixture resembles an icy paste.

2. Pour into two tall glasses to serve and top with a little cinnamon or grated nutmeg as well as fresh pieces of fruit.

Don Q Punch

There are many variations of rum punch across the Caribbean and this Puerto Rican punch is definitely a hit during the summer. It is super simple to make and uses Puerto Rico's own Don Q Rum.

Ingredients

1 ½ oz Don Q Gold rum

2 oz orange juice

¼ oz agave nectar

¾ oz orange juice

2 oz pineapple juice

1 tablespoon grenadine syrup

1 ½ oz Don Q Coco rum

¼ oz freshly squeezed lemon juice

½ oz ginger beer

1 orange peel (for garnish)

Preparation

1. Place all the ingredients into a cocktail shaker except the ginger beer and shake very well.

2. Strain the contents into a tall glass containing ice.

3. Top up with the ginger beer and add the orange peel as garnish.

Chichaito

This local favorite is common in bars and is generally available in shot-sized portions. Due to its highly alcoholic nature, this drink can certainly creep up on you and as the name suggests can result in you speaking uncontrollably, thus the meaning of its name, gossip. For this reason, some people choose to chill the drink and sip it slowly.

Ingredients

½ oz Light Rum

1 oz anisette liqueur

2 drops lemon juice

Preparation

1. Into a small shot glass, add the rum and anisette then two drops of lemon juice.

2. Enjoy as a shot.

Helpful Tip

If you prefer to sip this drink slowly, increase the ingredient amounts proportionately and serve on the rocks.

Bili

Vieques, which is an island of Puerto Rico, has Bili as its official alcoholic beverage. It is most popular in the summer and is made from the flesh of the quenepa fruit. In other islands, the fruit is known as chenette, guinep, mamoncillo, genip or Spanish lime just to name a few. There is an official Bili festival which is held in July, the height of summer.

Ingredients

8 cups white rum

2 ½ lbs quenepas

1 ½ cups brown sugar

½ teaspoon vanilla

1 stick cinnamon

Preparation

1. Split the quenepa skins open, remove the fruit and place into a container.

2. Add the vanilla and sugar then mix.

3. Continue to mix to ensure all of the sugar has dissolved.

4. Add the rum, a little at a time while mixing until all of it has been added.

5. Do a taste test and add more sugar if desired.

6. Add the cinnamon stick and pour all the contents into a bottle, close tightly and store.

Helpful Tip

Typically the bottle in which the bili has been poured, is wrapped and buried in a hole in the ground, from anywhere from a month to a year.

Mavi

Most commonly known as Mauby, this bittersweet drink is made from the bark and in some cases the fruit of the Mavi tree. Enjoyed whether still or fizzy, Mavi is popular for its diuretic properties and can be fermented, if desired. This recipe will show you how to make the fermented version.

Ingredients

1 oz mavi bark

1 oz ginger root

1 cinnamon stick

12 ½ cups water

2 ½ cups granulated sugar

2 ½ cups brown sugar

Preparation

1. In a cup and a half of water, boil the bark, ginger and cinnamon stick for five minutes.

2. After the time has elapsed, strain the liquid and allow it to cool completely.

3. In a separate deep container, dissolve the sugars into eleven cups of the water, then add the strained Mavi liquid, mixing until a foam forms.

4. Decant the liquid into glass bottles and seal them moderately (not too tightly) with cloth plugs.

5. Place the bottles in direct sunlight for four to six hours, then refrigerate until very cold.

Helpful Tips

Mavi tastes much better the colder it is. If making the still version, just refrigerate the bottles without placing them in the sun.

Watermelon Sangria

This traditional Spanish punch has a mixture of fruit, wine and alcohol or other juice. It's a great summer cooler and a hit when entertaining a large number of guests.

Ingredients

2 lbs seedless watermelon cubes

½ lb watermelon balls, on skewers

1 bottle white wine, dry

6 oz vodka

4 oz cointreau or triple sec

4 oz citrus syrup

Ice

Preparation

1. Puree the watermelon cubes then strain into a jug.

2. Pour in the wine, vodka, syrup and Cointreau, stir, then refrigerate for no less than two hours.

3. Before serving, stir again, then pour into wine glasses filled with ice.

4. Use the skewered watermelon balls to garnish the glasses.

Tembleque Latte

This hot beverage features a harmonious blend of coconut and coffee flavors in the form of a creamy latte. The hint of cinnamon rounds out the flavor in a lovely way and you will enjoy having this treat with your morning breakfast or noon meal.

Ingredients

1 espresso shot, brewed

1 ½ oz coconut-flavored syrup

4 oz milk

Pinch cinnamon powder

Preparation

1. Mix the espresso shot and syrup together in a coffee mug and set aside.

2. Place the milk to heat up in a small pot on a medium to low heat and when it just begins to boil, add to the mixture in the mug and stir.

3. Top with a sprinkling of cinnamon and serve.

Rum Horchata

Horchata is the name given to a variety of beverages made from plant-based milks. As a result, horchata can be made from various nuts, seeds or grains. It generally has a creamy appearance and can be flavored with spices of your choice.

Ingredients

4 cups milk

1 stick cinnamon

½ cup rice flour

14 oz condensed milk

2 tsp vanilla extract

½ cup spiced rum

Ice cubes

Preparation

1. Bring the milk and cinnamon stick to a low simmer on a medium heat.

2. Remove the pot and pour the contents into a glass bowl.

3. Add the condensed milk, flour and vanilla, whisking until properly mixed, then refrigerate until completely cool.

4. Strain the cooled liquid through a cheesecloth to remove the flour.

5. Add the rum, stir, pour into a glass containing ice then enjoy.

Café con Leche

Puerto Rican coffee is hailed as one of the best in the world, with its potent and full-bodied flavor. With this recipe you will find that the key to making excellent café con leche is due to proportions. The coffee to water ratio is 1 tablespoon coffee to 1 cup water, while the milk is ¼ cup for each coffee cup, with just a teaspoon of sugar for each cup. The result is a very bold brew.

Ingredients

2 tablespoons ground coffee, heaped

2 cups water

½ cup milk

2 teaspoons sugar

Preparation

1. Place the water in a saucepan and when it begins to simmer add the coffee.

2. Stir constantly for a minute while still simmering then turn off the heat to allow the coffee to steep for a minute or two. Stir once or twice as it rests.

3. Using a coffee sock, strain the coffee into a pot.

4. Using a saucepan, add the milk and sugar. Place on the stove and stir to dissolve the sugar.

5. Once the milk starts to foam, pour the coffee from the pot into the saucepan and let it simmer.

6. Serve the coffee in cups and enjoy.

Refresco de Tamarindo

It is not surprising that across the Caribbean you will find similarities in food and drink, as some of the flora and fauna are similar. The Tamarind drink is a beverage also made in Jamaica. The Puerto Rican version adds more spices, making use of cloves and/or star anise and some recipes also feature cinnamon and ginger. Carbonated water can be added for fizz. if desired.

Ingredients

½ pound peeled tamarind

3 cup water

1 cup dark sugar

1 stick cinnamon

4 cloves or star anise

Preparation

1. Put the water in a container and add the tamarinds, leaving them to soak for one hour along with the cinnamon stick and cloves or star anise.

2. Wash hands well, then squish the tamarinds removing the seeds.

3. Strain the liquid into a jug then add the sugar to sweeten.

4. Chill in the refrigerator and serve with ice.

Helpful Tips

If the drink is too sour you may dilute with additional water.

The cinnamon stick and star anise or cloves can be transferred to the jug and stored in the juice as it chills in the fridge, for a stronger spice flavor.

Sweet Cinnamon Horchata

This particular version of horchata is made using old fashioned rolled oats and spiced with cinnamon. This is a great way for vegans or those that are lactose intolerant to enjoy a creamy drink, without the dairy.

Serves 4

Ingredients

1 cup rolled oats

1 cinnamon stick, cracked into small pieces

4 cup water

Sugar or agave syrup to sweeten

Preparation

1. Soak the oats and cinnamon in the water for no less than half an hour.

2. After soaking, blend the entire mixture then strain into a pitcher.

3. Sweeten the liquid as desired with the agave syrup or sugar then chill before serving.

Helpful Tip

If serving right away, use ice cubes.

Gasolina

This potent alcoholic cocktail is made up of various types of alcoholic beverages in shot quantities, then topped off with fruit juices or sprite soda. It is usually enjoyed in shot sized portions, as it is wise to be careful of the sheer strength of the components.

Ingredients

1 shot of gin

1 shot of white rum

1 shot of white tequila

1 shot of vodka

Sprite

Preparation

1. Add all the shots into a tall drinking glass then top up with the sprite.

2. Serve gasolina in shot glasses.

Mojito

The origin of the mojito is uncertain however this cocktail has become a well-loved Puerto Rican favorite and is a regular feature in resorts and bars. The minty and tangy flavor is ideal for hot summer days or cool party nights. With just the right amount of rum, this drink pleases every time.

Ingredients

For simple syrup

1 cup water

1 cup sugar

10-15 spearmint leaves

For mojito

1 oz mint-infused simple syrup

1 – 1 ½ oz lime juice

10-15 spearmint leaves

2 oz light rum

Club soda

Crushed ice

Preparation

1. To make the simple syrup, combine the sugar and water in a saucepan and stir while heating until all the sugar has dissolved.

2. Turn the heat off then add the first set of mint leaves and steep for an hour.

3. Strain the leaves, allow to cool, then use.

4. Combine the syrup, lime juice and mint leaves in a glass and muddle gently with a pestle. (Do not grind the leaves; simply bruise them to release the flavor).

5. Next add some crushed ice, muddle a little more, then add the rum.

6. Top the glass with ice then add a small amount of club soda, stir then serve.

Cuba Libre

Cuba Libre, which means 'Free Cuba', is a strange name for a drink to be considered as Puerto Rican. However, this is more than just a rum and coke, lime juice is also added which transforms a standard rum and coke into a Cuba Libre, coupled with the fact that the rum used is Puerto Rico's own Don Q. White rum can also be used, however aged dark rum adds more character. This is a popular cocktail in bars and restaurants and is very simple to make. Perfect for entertaining guests in the afternoon or evening.

Ingredients

Ice cubes

¼ glass of Don Q rum

½ lime

Coca Cola

Preparation

1. Place the ice in a drinking glass and add the rum quarter of the way.

2. Squeeze the half lime into the rum, top up with Coca Cola and serve.

43 con Leche

This Puerto Rican favourite is so delightfully simple to make. It is sweet and creamy and can be compared to a white Russian cocktail. It is quite popular on the bar scene and effortless to whip up at home.

Ingredients

1 ½ oz Licor 43 orange flavored liqueur

3 oz cold milk

Ice cubes

Cinnamon powder for garnish (optional)

Preparation

1. Add three cubes of ice to a glass followed by the Licor 43.

2. Pour on the milk.

3. If desired sprinkle a little cinnamon powder on the surface of the drink before serving.

Helpful Tip

Serve this beverage with a swizzle stick to enable even mixing of the liqueur, or mix before serving.

Ponche de Malta

This next Puerto Rican favourite is a non-alcoholic beverage which modifies plain malta with the addition of egg yolks and sugar. Malta is a carbonated, malted beverage with a bitter flavor and is an acquired taste for some people. With the sugar adding sweetness, it becomes more palatable for those who do not care for the original flavor.

Ingredients

1 egg yolk

1 cold Malta (can or bottle)

½ cup granulated sugar

Preparation

1. Combine the egg yolk and sugar and beat them until the mixture becomes a pale or almost white color.

2. Slowly add the malta, mix well and serve in suitable glassware.

Helpful Tip

Since this recipe calls for quite extensive beating of the egg yolk and sugar, you may opt to use a hand mixer instead.

Pina Colada

Probably the most famous of all Puerto Rican beverages, this drink was accidentally created, or rather created out of a dire need, by Ricardo Garcia, who was a coconut plantation owner, and a Caribbean resident originating from Barcelona. In 1914, the coconut workers on his plantation went on a strike. He was stretched for ingredients to make cocktails for his guests and decided to try his hand at mixing the pineapple juice with coconut cream and rum and poured the concoctions into hollowed pineapples. This proved to be a hit and now, his invention is probably the most famous cocktail invention ever.

Ingredients

3 oz (3 parts) Pineapple juice

1 oz (one part) White rum

1 oz (one part) Coconut cream

Preparation

1. In a blender, add pineapple juice, coconut cream and white rum. Blend for 20-30 seconds or until smooth. Serve cool.

Conclusion

Having re-created these classic Puerto Rican drinks, I'm sure you'll agree that Puerto Rican beverages combine individual ingredients in the most interesting way to produce some truly unique taste sensations.

The aim of this book was to focus on the very best and popular drinks from a range of different categories, allowing you to be able to select a drink for whichever occasion you require. Whether for a meal, entertaining friends or family, relaxing, or for the holidays, Puerto Rican beverages are flexible and effortless to make. I am sure that you will have discovered new preferences and re-created old favorites that bring great memories flooding back!

Why not add some great tasting Caribbean cocktail recipes by grabbing a copy of my other book; **Cocktails Cookbook**

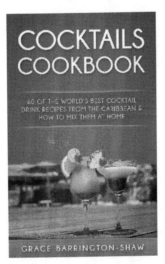

Just a reminder...don't forget to visit **www.ffdrecipes.com** for your FREE bonus cookbooks and to get exclusive access to our VIP World Recipes Club, which provides FREE book offers, discounts and recipe ideas!

Thank you.

Measurements & Conversions

US to Metric Corresponding Measures

Metric	Imperial
3 teaspoons	1 tablespoon
1 tablespoon	1/16 cup
2 tablespoons	1/8 cup
2 tablespoons + 2 teaspoons	1/6 cup
4 tablespoons	1/4 cup
5 tablespoons + 1 teaspoon	1/3 cup
6 tablespoons	3/8 cup
8 tablespoons	1/2 cup

10 tablespoons + 2 teaspoons	2/3 cup
12 tablespoons	3/4 cup
16 tablespoons	1 cup
48 teaspoons	1 cup
8 fluid ounces (fl oz)	1 cup
1 pint	2 cups
1 quart	2 pints
1 quart	4 cups
1 gallon (gal)	4 quarts
1 cubic centimeter (cc)	1 milliliter (ml)
2.54 centimeters (cm)	1 inch (in)
1 pound (lb)	16 ounces (oz)

Liquid to Volume

Metric	Imperial
15ml	1 tbsp
55 ml	2 fl oz
75 ml	3 fl oz
150 ml	5 fl oz (¼ pint)
275 ml	10 fl oz (½ pint)
570 ml	1 pint
725 ml	1 ¼ pints
1 litre	1 ¾ pints
1.2 litres	2 pints
1.5 litres	2½ pints
2.25 litres	4 pints

Weight Conversion

Metric	Imperial
10 g	½ oz
20 g	¾ oz
25 g	1 oz
40 g	1½ oz
50 g	2 oz
60 g	2½ oz
75 g	3 oz
110 g	4 oz
125 g	4½ oz
150 g	5 oz
175 g	6 oz
200 g	7 oz
225 g	8 oz
250 g	9 oz
275 g	10 oz

350 g	12 oz
450 g	1 lb
700 g	1 lb 8 oz
900 g	2 lb
1.35 kg	3 lb

G

Abbreviations

Abbreviation	Description
tsp	teaspoon
Tbsp	tablespoon
c	cup
pt	pint
qt	quart
gal	gallon
wt	weight
oz	ounce
lb	pound
g	gram
kg	kilogram
vol	volume

ml	milliliter
l	liter
fl oz	fluid ounce